Dear Mom, thank you
with all my heart

pictures and verse
by
Sandra Magsamen

EDITIONS

You are the best mother in the whole universe.

Your love makes me feel like a star.

Your
guidance helps
me
to soar...

and like a
seed I grow
because I am
lovingly
cared for.

You

teach me

to follow

my dreams...

and that true beauty comes from the heart.

You
celebrate
my
uniqueness...

and give me courage to make difficult choices.

Thank you for
understanding
and accepting
my decisions
although we
sometimes
disagree...

for
gently picking
me up
when I
fall...

and turning my tears into laughter.

Even
when we
don't see
eye to eye
we see
heart to heart.

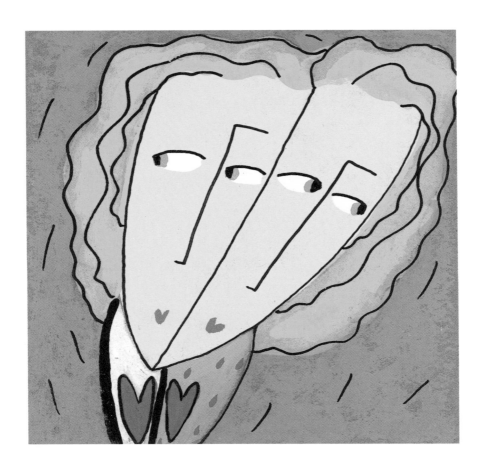

I'm grateful you are always there . . .

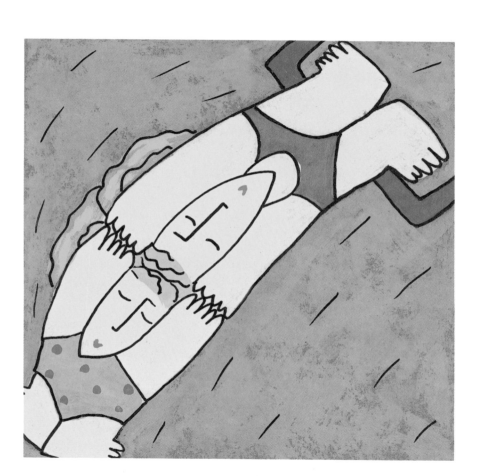

and because you believe in me, I believe in me.

I

love

you.

Pictures and verse by Sandra Magsamen
© 1999 Hanny Girl Productions, Inc.
Exclusive licensing agent Momentum Partners, Inc., NY, NY

S Editions is an imprint of SMITHMARK Publishers.

This edition published in 1999 by SMITHMARK Publishers, a division
of U.S. Media Holdings, Inc., 115 West 18th Street, New York, NY 10011

S Editions book are available for bulk purchase for sales promotion and premium use.
For details write or call the manager of special sales, S Editions,
115 West 18th Street, New York, NY 10011; 212-519-1215.

Distributed in the U.S. by Stewart, Tabori & Chang, a division of
U.S. Media Holdings, Inc., 115 West 18th Street, New York, NY 10011.

ISBN: 1-55670-896-3
Printed in Hong Kong

10 9 8 7 6 5 4 3 2 1